INTERNET MARKETING JOINT VENTURES

FINDING STRATEGIC ALLIANCES FOR BUSINESS PROFITS

ANTHONY EKANEM

Copyright © Anthony Ekanem
All Rights Reserved.

ISBN 978-1-68509-054-8

This book has been published with all efforts taken to make the material error-free after the consent of the author. However, the author and the publisher do not assume and hereby disclaim any liability to any party for any loss, damage, or disruption caused by errors or omissions, whether such errors or omissions result from negligence, accident, or any other cause.

While every effort has been made to avoid any mistake or omission, this publication is being sold on the condition and understanding that neither the author nor the publishers or printers would be liable in any manner to any person by reason of any mistake or omission in this publication or for any action taken or omitted to be taken or advice rendered or accepted on the basis of this work. For any defect in printing or binding the publishers will be liable only to replace the defective copy by another copy of this work then available.

Contents

Preface   v

1. Before Recruiting Joint Venture Partners   1
2. Things Your Potential Partner Looks For   4
3. Approaching And Recruiting Partners   7

Preface

A **Joint Venture** (in Internet Marketing) is defined as *"mutually beneficial cooperation between website owners"*. Many times, Internet Marketing Joint Ventures are entered into between an individual who has developed a new or innovative product or service and an established Internet Marketer who has spent considerable time developing their mailing list and their reputation. This type of agreement is a **win-win** situation.

The Joint Venture gives the developer of the new product or service access to potential customers that they would not otherwise have access to and the experienced Internet Marketer gains access to new products or services that the members of their list can benefit from. Both the product/service developer and the established Internet Marketer make a profit that neither of them would have made without the other and that is the very essence of the Joint Venture.

By joining forces and combining resources, skills and talents, a Joint Venture allows all parties to achieve more than anyone of them could have achieved alone. The fact is that Joint Venture is one of the jealously guarded secrets of successful Internet Marketers. Joint Ventures are certainly not a new concept. They have been around since the beginning of Internet Marketing.

For any marketer, new or seasoned, the Joint Venture is the quickest way to making a profit on low-cost or in most cases, even **FREE**. Often, even very well-established Internet Marketers will enter a Joint Venture enterprise, even those who are in direct competition with one another (well, believe it!). Why would competitors ever agree to a

Joint Venture? You may ask.

The answer is simple: Joint Ventures are profitable undertakings, and even competitors can make a profit by taking advantage of them. No marketer enters into a Joint Venture to help their competition. They enter into it to help themselves. As the saying goes, *"I eliminate my enemies by making friends"*!

At first glance, a Joint Venture agreement looks a bit daunting, but it is very simple. A Joint Venture joins the customers, advertising, products, services, knowledge, and skills of one website owner with those of another website owner for a specific project. Joint Venture agreements can be entered between two or more website owners or internet marketers.

Let us assume that an established Internet Marketer develops or acquires the rights to a product or service that would be beneficial to their customers. They could sell that product or service only to their list and make a nice profit. However, by entering into a Joint Venture agreement with other website owners who have lists of potential customers that would be interested in the same product or service, they could multiply their sales many times over. The owners of the other websites get the opportunity to recommend the product to their lists and make a profit as well. Everybody wins.

The Joint Venture works for both the established Internet Marketers and newcomers to the Internet Marketing scene. Established Internet Marketers are always looking for new or innovative products and services that can help their customers. By approaching an established Internet Marketer with a Joint Venture proposal, many newcomers have gotten their start.

CHAPTER ONE

Before Recruiting Joint Venture Partners

The old saying, *"Put your money where your mouth is"*, is used to challenge someone to gamble on themselves and what they believe they can achieve. A great idea has no value until it is backed up with an investment of hard work and money and carried to fruition.

Until you have invested your own time, effort, energy, and money into your idea, it is a good bet that nobody else is going to invest anything in it. You may have an idea about a product or service that you are sure will sell like crazy in a certain niche on the Internet. However, to get that product or service sold, you must invest in yourself and your idea.

You will need to do the necessary research to determine if the idea is feasible and if there is a market for the product or service you want to sell. You may need to acquire some software or information products to help you create your product or service. Creating a product or service can take a substantial investment of time, effort, money and energy.

When you approach a well-established Internet Marketer with your idea and a Joint Venture plan, they will first want to know how much you have invested in your business. If you do not believe in yourself and your product or service, they will not believe in your business either. They will want to know how much of your time, effort, energy and money you have invested before they can decide how much of their resources they are willing to invest in it. The *rule of thumb is:* **invest in yourself, so others will be willing to invest in you.**

Many times, a beginner Internet Marketer would approach an established Internet Marketer with a Joint Venture proposal only to receive negative feedback. The inexperienced marketer often feels like they just got blown off and that the experienced marketer did not take the time to hear them out. However, that is not the most likely case. Successful and experienced Internet Marketers are very busy people. They most likely work more hours every day than others do.

These successful men and women do not have a starting or closing time built into their business. They probably dream about their jobs when they are asleep. When one of them is approached with a Joint Venture proposal, they will undoubtedly be interested. Joint Ventures are their bread and butter. They have twenty-four hours in a day just like every other person.

As a new Internet Marketer, it would be wise to approach an experienced and successful Internet Marketer with a Joint Venture proposal that they can see will make them money and not require hours of their valuable time. Do all the research regarding your product or service's marketability. Show that there is a market for your product or service as it relates to their mailing lists. Your proposal needs to be short and straightforward, and your sales letter needs to be top-notch.

The main thing to remember is that successful Internet Marketers are busy people and "I do not have time" does not mean, "I will never have time". Another school of thought suggests that the same words can also mean "that is not where my business is heading" or "your Joint Venture proposal is not important enough to be at the top of my priority list".

CHAPTER TWO

Things Your Potential Partner Looks For

A Joint Venture partnership with an established Internet Marketer is the swiftest path to success for the new Internet Marketer or an individual who has created a product or service but has never done any Internet Marketing before. Partnering with an established internet marketer gives the new marketer instant credibility and access to the best market for their product or service.

When approaching an experienced Internet Marketer with a Joint Venture proposal, you should realise that there are three main things the marketer will weigh when determining whether to accept your Joint Venture proposal, namely:

1. **The Product Quality** will be considered and looked at critically from all angles. The experienced Internet Marketer will not recommend an inferior product or service to their mailing list. They have put a great deal of time and effort into establishing themselves as reliable and dependable providers of information. An inferior product or service can undo all their hard work. Check what you are offering to ensure it is of high quality and

that it delivers what is promised.

2. **The Market** for the product or service has been well established. You must have done your research and be able to prove to him that there is a market for the product or service you are selling. No matter how great your new buggy whip might be, there will not be a market for it and no demand either. What you are selling must be relevant to today's marketplace.

3. **How persuasive your sales letter is** will be the last determining factor. Even if you have a high-quality product or service for which you have established that there is a market and a demand, if your sales letter is weak, the established Internet Marketer will not bother with you.

IMPORTANT TIP:

The thing about finding an internet marketing Joint Venture partner is that they need to be the right partner; someone who has a list of potential customers who will need or want the product or service you are offering. For example, if you have developed a new chemical for cleaning a house, it will not do much good to approach a company or an individual who sells swimming pool chemicals for partnership. Both products may be chemicals, but that is where the similarities end and their customers are not going to be in the market for what you are offering. Instead, it would help if you approached a company or an individual who sells house cleaning chemicals. They are the ones who already have the customers that you need to sell your product.

The same is true for all Internet Marketing. A marketer who has a list that they give financial advice to will not be interested in an e-Book about pet care. Submitting such a proposal is a complete waste of their time and yours. Look at the product or service you are offering and determine the market it would best serve and contact an established Internet Marketer in that niche. If you have a well-written and informative e-Book on pet care, the potential Joint Venture partner that you are most likely to find willing to join you will be selling closely related products or services. Their customers are the ones that are most likely to buy your eBook.

CHAPTER THREE

Approaching and Recruiting Partners

If you have created a good product or service and have all the bugs worked out and you have set up your website to promote and sell your product or service, the next step is to find affiliate marketers and Joint Venture partners to promote your product or service for you.

Affiliate marketing and Joint Venture agreements are the two biggest forms of Internet Marketing. When you join the two, you get a real big deal. The place to find Joint Venture partners on the internet is https://www.delavo.com/. You can find individuals and corporations there who are also looking for Joint Venture partners. You need to have already set up your affiliate marketing programme and have affiliate some marketers signed up with you to promote your products or service.

The idea here is to find individuals or companies (affiliate marketers) who will promote and sell your product or service for you on a commission basis and then find Joint Venture partners that will combine with the affiliate marketers to promote your products or services to their lists of potential consumers.

Once your affiliate marketing programme is up and running, you will be in a better position to search for Joint Venture partners for your products and your affiliate marketers. You will want your Joint Venture partners to be happy with you. The happier they are with you, the harder they will work at promoting your products or services, which is the ultimate objective. The structure of your Joint Venture partner compensation package has much to do with how hard they will work at promoting your products or services.

Everyone involved in Joint Ventures and affiliate marketing programmes on the Internet knows about the **80/20 rule**; that is, 80% of sales are generated by 20% of affiliates and Joint Venture partners. Just think about it: if you can beat that **80/20** rule by even a little margin, your sales would explode. And with a good Joint Venture compensation package, you can make that happen.

The first thing you should do, of course, is to set up the programme to make everything for your Joint Venture partners. Make it quick and easy for them to locate your affiliate links, advert copies, banners, and other tools. You also need to provide login details and other important links in every email you send out to them.

Know what commission or profit splits you can live with and be as generous as possible with your affiliate and joint venture partners. You may need to run contests with prizes based on the number of sales to be reached at the end of the contest.

You may think that commissions, contest prizes and even profit splits may be enough. But there is one more thing you can add to your Joint Venture compensation plan that can turn the tide for you, and that is a promise to co-promote their offers after your launch period is over.

Your Joint Venture partners are the fuel for your product launch. They need to be happy with your compensation plan such that they are willing to give your products or services their full attention.

After identifying your prospective Joint Venture partners, the next thing is to contact them. Many times, it is only the email address of your potential Joint Venture partners that is available on their website. Remember that they most likely receive several emails every day, so you need to construct your email in a way that will attract their attention. This is not the right place to take shortcuts. Open your prospective Joint Venture partners' website as you write your email to them.

There was a celebrated advertising slogan which read "set it and forget it". That was a great idea, but it does not work with Joint Venture partners. They are never set, and you better not forget them, otherwise, they will forget about you too.

You can select prospective Joint Venture partners and do the initial email campaigns. Sales will pour in, and the world will take on a healthy glow, but after a few days or weeks, sales can fall to zero. There is no point starting with all new Joint Venture partners. That will consume too much time and energy. The best thing to do is to motivate the joint venture partners you already have to continue promoting your products or services.

Here are some ideas that you can use to keep your Joint Venture partners working for you:

1. Send them articles they can send out in their mailings that include your product links. The articles can also be embedded in their articles on their website. Remember that website owners are always looking for quality and

unique contents.

2. Do a special report they can offer to their subscribers or something they can make available as a download from their website or blog.

3. Write a mini-course they can put on their autoresponder with links to your products.

4. Send them banner adverts for their website or blog.

5. Audio and video are a big deal, and they are getting bigger on the Internet these days. You may even consider creating an audio or video product for them to use on their website or blog.

Make sure that you keep your Joint Venture partners highly motivated, inspired, and well-armed with marketing tools so that they will continue to promote your products or services weeks, months or maybe years after the launch date.

JOINT VENTURE SUCCESS TIPS

Before you approach a potential Joint Venture partner, here are some tips on what you need to do and do them well. These are:

1. **Perfect your product or service.** Work all the bugs out. Your product or service needs to do what it promises to do.

2. **Research** to be sure that there is a demand for your product or service.

3. **Invest in yourself**. You should have worked hard to build your credibility.

Once you have accomplished all the above and have located some Joint Venture partners to help you launch your product or service, there are things you must do to get the most out of your product launch and beyond.

1. **Build a strong relationship with your Joint Venture partners.** Be sincere and honest in all your dealings with your joint venture partners and affiliates. Be friendly and get to know them on a personal level if possible.

2. **Look beyond your nose.** This relates to number one above. Do not see the product launch as a one-time deal. Consider it a stepping-stone to future launches and Joint Venture projects.

3. **Work hard before, during and after the product launch.** Do not be 'out to lunch' during the product launch period.

4. **Always be available at any hour of the day or night.** Problems happen, and you must stay in touch and be available to resolve any problem that may arise.

This is wishing you the very best as you strike your next Joint Venture deal for success.

www.ingramcontent.com/pod-product-compliance
Lightning Source LLC
Chambersburg PA
CBHW070847220526
45466CB00002B/919